# Eddie The Electron Moves Out

Melissa Rooney, Ph.D.
Illustrated by Harry Pulver Jr.

Amberjack Publishing
Chicago

AMBERJACK
PUBLISHING

Chicago

An imprint of Chicago Review Press Incorporated
814 North Franklin Street
Chicago, Illinois 60610
ISBN 978-1-944995-14-0

Eddie the Electron Moves Out

Publisher's Cataloging-in-Publication data

Names: Rooney, Melissa, author.
Title: Eddie the electron moves out / by Melissa Rooney.
Description: New York, NY: Amberjack Publishing, 2017.
Identifiers: ISBN 978-1-944995-14-0 | LCCN 2016959652
Summary: Eddie the Electron is finally out of his balloon, and now he's ready to move out into the upper reaches of the atmosphere.
Subjects: LCSH Electrons--Juvenile literature. | Atoms--Juvenile literature. | Matter--Properties--Juvenile literature. | Helium--Juvenile literature. | Atmospheric physics--Juvenile literature. | JUVENILE NONFICTION / Science & Nature / General
Classification: LCC QC793.5.E62 .R67 2017 | DCC 539.7--dc23

Printed in the United States of America

# Reviews for *Eddie the Electron*

"*Eddie the Electron* is a fun scientific exploration. Compelling images and engaging language take children on an atomic adventure...This book is a great addition to any classroom."

-Charlotte Peck,
Montessori Primary Teacher

"*Eddie the Electron* bounces with gusto from sub-atomic particles to planets, delivering core scientific concepts in a playful language. Lively illustrations help bring students along for the ride."

-Danielle Quattry Comer,
STEM Teacher
Mother of 2 preschool children

"How many children can be engaged with science because of a single publication? Melissa Rooney's achievement in creating *Eddie the Electron* is explaining the complexities of electrochemistry to the elementary mind in a delightful tale of a noble atomic particle."

-John Hale,
Co-owner of Binding Time,
Martinsville/Danville, VA

"*Eddie the Electron* is a great instructional resource for helping science come alive for young readers. It is a nice integration of science and literacy. It is a book that is appropriate for the school library, regular classroom, or your own child's bookshelf."

-Elizabeth Ragland,
5th-Grade Social Studies and English

"I bought the book with my 9 year old in mind, and I wasn't too sure my 5 year old would understand much. Boy was I wrong! My 5 year old LOVES the book and asks for it every night at bedtime so he can laugh out loud at the funny illustrations and cheer for Eddie to escape from Erwin, his boring orbit-mate. Meanwhile, my 9 year old impressed her teacher with her knowledge of electrons and protons, all after only one reading of the story. I would most definitely recommend this book to anyone with kids that like funny stories (and whose kids don't?)."

-Paige England Santmyer, parent

"This book is a fabulous introduction to science for kids. My boys, aged 10 and 8, loved it and afterwards talked for a long while about all the things they could imagine if they were an atom!! I agree with Melissa Rooney, the author—we often underestimate how much our children can understand and will be interested in. This book gives them that chance."

-Helen Canny, parent

"This humorous and educational diversion into the social lives of electrons was quite a hit with my 3 and 6 year olds! And I bet it sticks with them a lot longer than most science lessons. Way to make learning some difficult concepts simple and fun!"

-Jennifer Payne Bauer, parent

To my college analytical chemistry professor, Gary Rice, whose entertaining passion for chemistry led me to major in the subject.

# Note:

For more information about Eddie's atoms, look for the small numbers throughout the book. These are called *endnotes*. They tell you that there is more information (on the stuff you just read) at the end of the book.

On the last pages of the book, find each matching number and read the information beside it.

A lot of times *endnotes* are harder to understand than the story itself, but figuring them out is part of the fun, especially for a scientist!

# Hey there.

## Bet ya didn't think you'd hear from me again, right?

When I shot out of that balloon,[1] I expected to fly
to the end of the universe in an instant! But I'm
glad I didn't. It's been quite a ride.

1

I pinged all around the room, bumping into billions of other atoms every second.[2]

Then someone opened the windows, and *whoosh!* I was outside.

What a place! Cars and planes, trees and oceans, and don't even get me started on amusement parks!

As I was marveling at your world, I began to realize something:

I was surrounded—and I mean *surrounded*-by Nitrogen and Oxygen atoms.[3]

I bumped into an Argon or Carbon Dioxide molecule
from time to time, but Helium atoms were few and
far between.

The balloon I came from was *filled* with Helium atoms. I bumped into 7 billion of them every single second.[4] But once we are in the open air, we Helium atoms are outnumbered by about 200,000 to 1.

So I said to myself, "Whoa, Eddie. Let's think about this before we freak out."

I thought back to before I was put in my balloon and even before I was put into the metal tank used to fill that balloon. I thought back to when I was still stuck inside the Earth's crust.

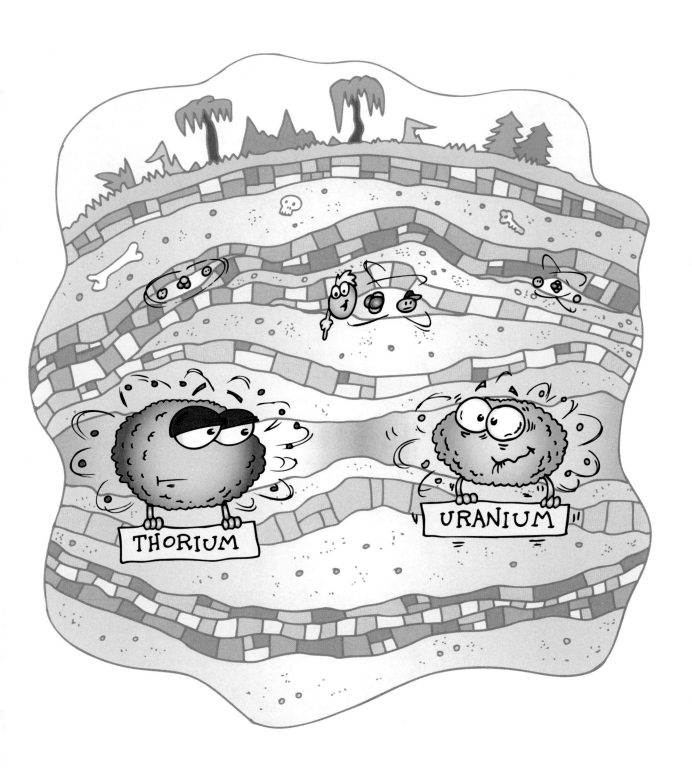

See, when Earth formed about 4.5 billion years ago,
two kinds of unstable atoms, Uranium and Thorium, were
trapped inside the crust.

When I say unstable, I don't mean on a daily basis.
These guys can be just as stable as you or me for
billions of years. But one day, when nobody's looking—
BOOM!—they self-destruct in a nuclear explosion.[5]

When the atomic dust settles, Helium is one of the leftover pieces.

Because it survives all the energy released in that explosion, Helium is *incredibly* stable and incredibly light. Even lighter than air. . . which makes me realize something else.

I'm rising. And fast. I can't even
see your house anymore.

I am sooooo much lighter than the air that I just keep
floating up above it. This is amazing . . .

But it means I'm going to have to speed up my story.

The Helium atom I lived in was formed a couple billion years ago. If you think being trapped in my balloon was boring, try being trapped under the earth's surface for a few billion years! I thought I would die of pair annihilation![6]

Then, one day, there was a tremendous noise, even louder than when the dinosaurs were tromping around up there. Before I knew what was happening, my Helium atom, and zillions of others, were going up, up, up, through the earth's crust into an endless array of metal tubes, until we got trapped in the metal tank that was used to fill my balloon.

Turns out that you humans mine Helium for all sorts
of things, but mostly for use as a "coolant"—to keep
things in laboratories and manufacturing plants from
overheating. Anyway, you guys need Helium for things
like welding, fiber optics, MRI scans, and even making
microchips for computers.

Which brings me to another issue. The way you guys use it, you may run out of Helium altogether in less than thirty years.

You see, Helium is what's called a "nonrenewable resource," because it takes billions of years to form under the earth's crust. Once you release Helium into the air . . . well, it's gone.

There's nothing to keep it from rising past the clouds and all the way to the outer reaches of Earth's atmosphere.

Speaking of which . . .

Wow. I'm high above Earth now.

It really is quite a marble . . . err, marvel.
Both actually.

Now that I am in the earth's upper atmosphere, I don't seem to be rising anymore. There are a lot more Helium atoms, which is a relief. If my time under the earth's crust is any indication, it looks like I could be here for a while.

Don't get me wrong. I'm not complaining. The view is incredible. There are lots of cool, colorful specks and flashes of light.

But mostly it's empty space. I could travel hundreds of miles without bumping into another atom.

The funny thing is, I'm not lonely at all.

It seems that I am not only surrounded by empty space; but that I'm actually a part of it. I don't understand it, but I think your man Einstein may have.

My fellow atoms and I have become connected in a way that surpasses space and time. Wait 'til you hear *their* stories.

But that'll have to wait for another time.

Until then, when you look up in the sky, think of me.

Oh! And you may want to skip the Helium balloons at your next party.

ENDNOTES:

1. Eddie and his orbit-mate, Erwin, are part of a Helium atom that was once trapped inside a grocery-store balloon. They, along with zillions of other Helium atoms, made the balloon float upward. In his first book, Eddie convinces the reader to pop the balloon so he can escape (*Eddie the Electron*, Amberjack Publishing).

2. Helium atoms like Eddie's move through the atmosphere at speeds greater than 3,000 miles per hour. That's a mighty fast pinball!

3. Most of Earth's atmosphere (including the air you breathe) is Nitrogen and Oxygen. When Helium atoms like Eddie's travel through the Earth's atmosphere, about 8 out of every 10 molecules they bump into (around 78%) are Nitrogen atoms. Two out of every 10 atoms (around 21%) are Oxygem atoms. In contrast, about 1 in every 100 atoms (1%) are Argon, and about 4 in 10,000 (0.036%) are Carbon Dioxide.

   But get this — only 5 out of every *1,000,000* atoms that Eddie bumps into (0.00052%) are Helium atoms. That's like you walking from one end of Dallas, Texas, to the other end and only seeing *one* other person.

4. On a nice summer day (around 77 degrees Fahrenheit) a single Helium atom in a typical party balloon is experiencing 7 *billion* collisions per second. This means that it bangs into 7,000,000,000 other Helium atoms every single second! Even if you clapped without stopping for a whole year, you couldn't clap your hands that many times.

5. Certain kinds of atoms can split into smaller atoms, though it can take them billions of years to do so. This is called nuclear fission. When it happens, it produces a lot of energy. Nuclear reactors use nuclear fission to make enough energy to power whole cities.

6. Until the 1900s, electrons were thought to be indestructible. But we now know that they can be destroyed (or *annihilated*) if they collide with a positron. This is called *pair annihilation.*

   A positron is the exact opposite of an electron. In fact, current science thinks that a positron is just an electron moving backward in time! So when a positron and an electron collide — *poof!* They annihilate each other, releasing energy in the form of light (2 or 3 photons of light, to be exact).

## About the Author

Before writing children's books, Melissa (Bunin) Rooney grew up in Martinsville, VA, attended the College of William and Mary, and earned her Ph.D. in Chemistry from the University of North Carolina.

One of her passions is introducing scientific concepts to children and fueling their interest, especially when they don't immediately understand. After all, the things we don't understand are the most intriguing, and contemplating them results in scientific and technological advances (not to mention employment!).

Find out more about Melissa at **www.melissarooneywriting.com**, or visit her on Facebook at **www.facebook.com/melissarooneywriting/**. And now you can visit Eddie on Facebook too: **https://www.facebook.com/EddieTheElectron/**.

## About the Illustrator

Harry Pulver Jr. has worked as a professional illustrator for over 30 years.

His clients include Crain's New York Business, The Wall Street Journal, Cargill Inc., Coca Cola, Microsoft, 3M, Sony/Epic Music Group, American Lung Assoc., Scholastic Inc., National Geographic World and The Children's Television Workshop.

He attended St. Olaf College, The Minnesota College of Art and Design, and Pratt Manhattan School of Design.

When he's not drawing, Harry also plays accordion in his award winning Polka Rock band, TUBBY ESQUIRE.

You can see more of his artwork or contact him at **www.harrypulver.com**.